Applied
Life Skills Studen

An online English tutoring service with

Applied ESL

a creative approch

Dara K. Fulton

Applied ESL Life Skills Student Workbook 4
Copyright © 2025 all rights reserved

Purpose of this workbook

The purpose of this workbook is for students to practice what they learn via video lessons and/or tutoring sessions. This workbook is the last one of the Applied ESL Life Skills student workbook series focusing on life skills and everyday English. Each exercise and activities are selected from topics based on lessons. Activities range from grammar, spelling, and vocabulary practice to reading and writing comprehension. Each activity is based on real-life scenarios that students can apply in their daily life. This workbook is not based on a particular English level. Instead, the lessons and exercises offer students an opportunity to review and practice their English skills.

Who is Dara K. Fulton?

Dara is the founder and ESL teacher of Applied ESL. Applied ESL is an online English tutoring service with a creative approach that helps adult learners build confidence while improving their English speaking skills. Her tutoring company focuses on the basic and intermediate levels of the English language through conversation, listening, and pronunciation practice with the use of visuals and real life scenarios. The goal is to help students feel confident to speak English in everyday life. Dara has years' experience teaching English as a Second Language (ESL) to adults. She is passionate about teaching and helping people.

Dara likes to tell her students, "Try your best."

Table of Contents

Preview: Alphabet and Numbers

The Alphabet

A a	B b	C c	D d
E e	F f	G g	H h
I i	J j	K k	L l
M m	N n	O o	P p
Q q	R r	S s	T t
U u	V v	W w	X x
Y y	Z z		

Numbers (1-10, 20-100)

One 1	Two 2	Three 3	Four 4	Five 5	Six 6	Seven 7	Eight 8	Nine 9	Ten 10
Eleven 11	Twelve 12	Thirteen 13	Fourteen 14	Fifteen 15	Sixteen 16	Seventeen 17	Eighteen 18	Nineteen 19	Twenty 20
Twenty-one 21	Twenty-two 22	Twenty-three 23	Twenty-four 24	Twenty-five 25	Twenty-six 26	Twenty-seven 27	Twenty-eight 28	Twenty-nine 29	Thirty 30

Forty 40	Fifty 50	Sixty 60	Seventy 70	Eighty 80	Ninety 90	One-hundred 100

Calendar

January 2025

Sunday	Monday	Tuesday	Wednesday	Thursday	Friday	Saturday
			1	2	3	4
5	6	7	8	9	10	11
12	13	14	15	16	17	18
19	20	21	22	23	24	25
26	27	28	29	30	31	

A calendar shows the month, year, days of the week, and dates.

Days of the week

Monday
Tuesday
Wednesday
Thursday
Friday
Saturday
Sunday

IMPORTANT! There are 7 days in a week. Monday to Friday is called *weekdays*. Saturday and Sunday are called *weekends*.

Abbreviations for days of the week

Monday	Mon
Tuesday	Tues
Wednesday	Wed
Thursday	Thurs
Friday	Fri
Saturday	Sat
Sunday	Sun

Months of the year

January	July
February	August
March	September
April	October
May	November
June	December

IMPORTANT! There are 12 months in a year.

Dates

February 2025

Sunday	Monday	Tuesday	Wednesday	Thursday	Friday	Saturday
						1
2	3	4	5	6	(7)	8
9	10	11	12	13	14	15
16	17	18	19	20	21	22
23	24	25	26	27	28	

What is today's date?

Today is **Friday, February 7.**

When we are saying the <u>date</u>, it is the ***day, month, and number*** of that day.

We also include the <u>year</u>: Today is **Friday, February 7, <u>2025</u>.**

There are different ways of writing dates

- Friday, February 7, 2025 (day, month, date, year)
- 2/7/2025 or 2/7/25 (month, date, year)
- 2-7-25

*In some countries, the date looks like this: 7/2/2025 (date, month, and year)

*Some years are called a **<u>leap year</u>** because there's an extra day in a month. 2024 was a leap year because in February there were 29 days in the month instead of 28 days.

Ordinals

Ordinals are numbers that are in a series of numbers. For example: **1st (first)**, **2nd (second)**, **3rd (third)**, **4th (fourth)**

The 'st' 'nd' 'rd' and 'th' means the place that number is within a series of numbers

February 2025

Sunday	Monday	Tuesday	Wednesday	Thursday	Friday	Saturday
						1
2	3	4	5	6	7	8
9	10	11	12	13	14	15
16	17	18	19	20	21	22
23	24	25	26	27	28	

We use ordinals when saying the date.
Example: Today is Friday, February **7th**.

Ordinal numbers

First 1st	Second 2nd	Third 3rd	Fourth 4th	Fifth 5th
Sixth 6th	Seventh 7th	Eighth 8th	Ninth 9th	Tenth 10th
Eleventh 11th	Twelfth 12th	Thirteenth 13th	Fourteenth 14th	Fifteenth 15th
Sixteenth 16th	Seventeenth 17th	Eighteenth 18th	Nineteenth 19th	Twentieth 20th

IMPORTANT!

Zero (0) is not an ordinal number. After numbers 1, 2, and 3, all numbers will end in 'th'. Example: Twenty-first (21st), Twenty-second (22nd), Twenty-third (23rd), Twenty-fourth (24th)…Thirtieth (30th), Thirty-first (31st).

Seasons

Seasons are different types of weather in a year. In many places there are 4 seasons: **winter**, **spring**, **summer**, and **fall** (also called *autumn*).

Winter **Spring**

Summer	**Fall (Autumn)**

How is the weather today?

Weather is how the day feels (hot, cold, wet, or dry) and the temperature of the day.

Temperature is the measure of hot and cold. It is in degrees either in Fahrenheit or Celsius.

*Depending on the country, temperature will be in Fahrenheit or in Celsius.

Example: The weather today is 40 ***degrees Fahrenheit***. It is ***cold*** and ***wet*** outside.

How is the weather?

It is **sunny**.

It is **cloudy**.

It is **snowy**.

It is **rainy**.

What is your favorite type of weather? Why?

_____

_____

Holidays

Holidays are special occasions we celebrate during the year. Each country has their own holidays. These are some holidays that are popular in the United States.

January

New Year's Day (Jan 1st)

Chinese New Year (Jan-Feb)

February

Valentine's Day (Feb 14th)

May

Memorial Day (May 31st)

July

Independence Day (Jul 4th)

September

Labor Day (First Monday in Sept.)

October

Halloween (Oct 31st)

November

Thanksgiving (between Nov 22nd to 28th)

December

Christmas (Dec 25th)

New Year's Eve (Dec 31st)

Birthday: The day a person is born. We celebrate birthdays in many ways. The most common way is by eating cake, going out with family or friends, and receiving flowers or gifts.

When is your birthday? _____

Time

Time is the hours and minutes in a day. There are 5 time periods in a day: **morning**, **afternoon**, **evening**, **night**, and **midnight**.

AM: morning
PM: afternoon, evening, and night

Twelve is special because it is the *start* and the *middle* of a day
Example: 12 midnight: morning (start of a new day)
12 noon: afternoon (midday, middle of the day)

We write 12 am for midnight and 12 pm for afternoon.

How do we say the time?

It is **3 pm.**   It is **12 pm** or It is **12 noon**.

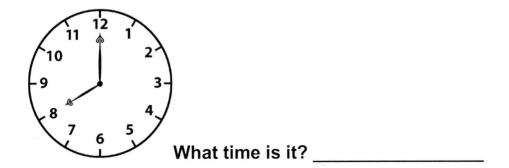

What time is it? _____

Formal and Informal English Greetings

What is the difference between formal and informal English greetings?

Formal English conversation is to speak in an official way using correct grammar and sentences. We speak formal English to people we usually don't know.

Example: Hello, how are you?

Informal English conversation is to speak in a free, relaxed way. It does not follow the correct rules of English. We speak informal English often and to people we know.

Example: Yo, what's up?

Both of these *greetings* mean the same thing. A **greeting** is the first, polite thing to say to someone.

How do you say hello?

We say hello in many INFORMAL ways. Some of the words we use are called <u>slang</u> because it's very informal and used to speak to people we know.

Formal	Informal
Hello	Hey
*Hi	Yo
How are you?	What's up?
How are you?	What's good?
How are you?	What's up with you?

*Hi is both formal and informal

Read the conversations

Formal

A: Hello, how are you?

B: I am fine, and you?

A: I'm okay.

Informal

A: Hey! What's up?

B: Hi, I'm good. You?

A: I'm chillin'.

We have informal ways of responding to greetings. We use *I'm* for informal responses.

Formal Response	Informal Response
I am (I'm) fine	*I'm good I'm alright
I am (I'm) happy	*I'm cool I'm chillin'
I am (I'm) okay	Nothing much
I am (I'm) tired	I'm sleepy
I am (I'm) so-so	I'm meh

I'm *good*, *alright*, *cool* and *chillin'* are used for saying I'm fine or I'm happy

Chillin' is very informal

Nothing much means nothing is happening or everything is okay

Meh is the same as so-so, which means not good or not bad

14

New York City Slang

What is slang?

Slang is informal English but more informal by the way we say words, expressions, and their meanings.

Slang is often considered "broken English" because it is how someone speaks it. The spelling of some slang words is not correct (example: chillin' instead of chilling).

Slang is spoken in different countries, cities, and neighborhoods. In New York City, USA there are many slang words and expressions. There are slang words used in each neighborhood of New York City!

New York City Slang Words and Expressions

What's up with you? (How are you? or Are you okay?)

I got you. (I am here for you.)

 **You frontin'** (You are trying to impress others, not being honest)

 **Don't sleep** (Pay attention)

 **Nah, I'm good.** (No, I'm fine.)

 **You feel me?** (Do you understand me? or Do you believe me?)

Do you know any slang words?

Write them here: _____

_____

DARA SAYS!

- ❖ Only use informal greetings to people you know or to someone who greets you informally. Informal greetings can be impolite to some people.
- ❖ Sometimes we use body language to speak informally. Body language means to use your body to speak. For example: waving
- ❖ Body language can help you feel confident to speak informal English.
- ❖ We use different slang words when talking to friends. For women, we say **sis** or **girl**. For men, we say **bro**, **hommie** or **my G**. My G means close friend.
- ❖ Only use these words to people you know. Some people may be offended if you call them *sis* or *hommie*.
- ❖ Attitude comes with using slang or informal English. The way you say these words and your body language, will make the communication clearer.
- ❖ In New York City, people appreciate it when you try to use slang or informal English. This is an easy way to help you practice your English, and feel comfortable talking to people.

Workplace Issues (Employment)

What are workplace issues?

Workplace issues are problems at the workplace. Let's look at some examples of workplace issues.

Harassment: behavior that intimidates or harass people

Unfair treatment: to be treated not in a fair way

Low pay: pay that is below average

Discrimination: unfair treatment towards people based on race, ethnicity, age, gender, religion, or disability

No work advancement: no opportunity to advance into a higher work position

Lunch break: time period to have lunch

Favoritism: to favor/show likeness to one person or group of people over others

Prejudice: to have a negative opinion about people of different backgrounds

Read the scenarios (situations) and write the vocabulary word (s) that best describes the scenario

- ❖ You ask your boss about an assignment and your boss says, "I don't understand you; can't you speak English?" _____
- ❖ You and your co-worker are applying for a higher position at the company. Your co-worker gets the position. She is 28 years old. You are 44. When you ask your

boss why you didn't get the position, he says, "She is younger and can do the job better." _____

❖ ABC Company offers a 1-hour lunch break for all employees except for those who work in departments 1 and 2. _____

❖ You worked at MV Store for 7 years. You only make $12/hour and ask your supervisor for a raise. You need to make more money for a new wheelchair. Your supervisor says, "Sorry, I can't give you a raise because of your disability. Just work more hours." _____

Read the article: *How to deal with a bad boss?* Answer the questions

"I hate my job!" Do you feel this way? Most people hate their jobs because of low pay, no work advancement, favoritism, and bad bosses! We've all had at least one bad boss in our work history. What makes a boss *bad*? A **bad boss** is a person who doesn't care about his employees. He or she focuses more on making money, and not the well-being of their workers. For example, Lilly comes to work every day, on-time, completes all of her assignments, and sometimes work during her lunch break. Unfortunately, Lilly doesn't make a lot of money, she doesn't receive **overtime**, and is often harassed by jealous co-workers. When Lilly complains to her boss about the work conditions, her boss says, "Oh please! Stop taking things so personal! You should be grateful I hired a woman." Lilly feels upset and alone. No one listens to her. She is the only woman at the company, and is denied work advancement. The boss favors the men and every six months they receive a raise. They get days off, and are allowed 1 hour lunch breaks. Lilly only gets a 45-minute lunch break. Eventually, Lilly **resigns** from this job. She **files a complaint** to her boss's boss. Do you think Lilly handled the situation well?

TRUE or FALSE

1- Lilly is happy at her job. _____

2- A bad boss is someone who cares about his/her employees. _____

3- Lilly is loved by her co-workers. _____

4- Overtime means to work after work hours. _____

5- Lilly's boss is prejudice. _____

6- Lilly stays at her job. _____

7- **File a complaint** means to let a boss know that something is wrong or something was done to you at work. _____

Letter of Complaint

A letter of complaint is a letter to a supervisor or a boss about something that you are dissatisfied with at the job, or something that happened to you at the workplace.

Read the letter of complaint and answer the questions

April 22, 2025

Dear Mr. Martinez and Ms. James,

I am writing this letter to inform you about the reason I left Better Security Inc. During my 5 years working there, I experienced prejudice, discrimination, harassment from co-workers, and low pay. I was the only woman in Department 3A and weren't allowed to have the same lunch break with my co-workers. They had a 1-hour lunch break and I only had 45 minutes. When I explained my concerns to my supervisor, he ignored me and said, "You should be lucky I hired a woman." I felt disrespected and angry. I asked for a higher salary and was denied. I tried to transfer to another department, but was told they didn't need me. I felt frustrated, disrespected, and discriminated against. I wanted to bring this to your attention, because I don't want this to happen to someone else. I hope you speak to my supervisor and his staff about their treatment towards women. It is not fair and should not be tolerated.

Thank you for reading my letter.

Sincerely,

Lilly Chan

1-Who wrote the letter of complaint? _____

2-Who is the letter addressed to? _____

3-What were some of the problems the former employee experienced?

_____

_____

4-Why is it important to write a letter of complaint?

_____

_____

_____

Read the problem and write a complaint letter to Mr. Mohammad

You are an employee at Shine Bright Jewelry Store. You have been working there for 10 years. You love selling jewelry to customers. You were promoted to supervisor last year. Your boss, Mr. Ahmed left and his cousin Mr. Fawaz took his place. Mr. Fawaz is not patient and yells at you for making any mistakes. He likes to interrupt you when you talk to customers. He is not pleasant and makes fun of you, because you don't speak Arabic well. You speak English and Spanish. You have a good salary, but recently asked Mr. Fawaz for vacation time. He said no. Mr. Fawaz takes time off when he wants, but you can only request time off twice a month. You don't want to quit your job, but you don't like what is happening. You write a complaint letter to Mr. Mohammad. He is the owner of the jewelry store.

Date_____

Dear Mr. Mohammad,

Sincerely,

Your name _____

21

DARA SAYS!

- ❖ Always remain calm in difficult situations at work. It's not easy, but it will prevent you from getting in trouble or getting fired.
- ❖ Always let your supervisor or boss know what is going on. If it is your boss or supervisor that's causing the problem, inform the next person in charge. In big companies there are several supervisors (example: supervisor of the department of sales)
- ❖ Try not to overreact or lose your temper. This will result in arguments or termination (get fired from a job)
- ❖ Always write down any incidents that occurs. This is your proof to show a supervisor or boss when filing a complaint
- ❖ If you decide to resign from your job, always write a resignation letter explaining your reason

Ways to Study (Education)

How to study?

To study means to review any lesson or new things you learned in class. Studying can be challenging, because it takes concentration, time, and patience. Many people prefer to sit in a quiet place such as, a library, at home, or a café that's not too noisy.

How do YOU study? Look at the pictures and match the correct letter with the picture

a. type notes on a phone and listen to text-to-voice (computer reads notes)

_____

b. highlight class notes

_____

c. flashcards

_____

Learning English is hard because you have to learn many different things. For example, grammar, new words, spelling, pronunciation, reading, and writing. There are so many rules! It's hard to remember them all...

d. notebook with class notes

———————

Which one of these study techniques do you use?

_____

_____

_____

Read the checklist and answer the questions

1- Organize your notes for each class
Use a notebook or a binder to organize your notes for each class

2- Set a study schedule
Pick a day (s) and time (s) to study. This will keep you organized and motivated.

Example:
Study English Monday to Wednesday
9:00 am- 10:00 am
Study math Tuesday, Thursday and Saturday
3:00 pm- 5:00 pm

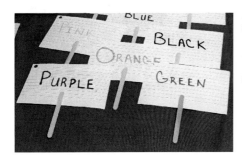

3- Use flashcards
Flashcards (also called index cards) are cards you use to write notes, words, or anything that you are studying.

4- <u>Find a quiet place to study</u>

This can be a room in your house, or a library. Some people like to study in a park or a cafe but there are distractions. Some people listen to music when studying. It all depends on what is comfortable for you.

5- <u>Study groups</u>

You can study with other people and help each other with questions.

6- <u>Take breaks!</u> Always take time to relax.

What do you study?

_____

How do you study?

_____

_____

What do you *want* to study? Why?

_____

_____

_____

You Try: Create a study schedule
You are studying English. Write a study schedule. Use the checklist to help you.

Write down 3 ways you will study

_____

_____

_____

Do you like to study Why or why not?

DARA SAYS!

- ❖ Always take breaks when you are studying
- ❖ Drink water and eat something before you study. It will help you to concentrate. Never study on an empty stomach
- ❖ Reward yourself by doing something nice. For example, buy something you like or go outside for a walk. Studying is not easy
- ❖ Don't be too hard on yourself. Studying something new is hard and takes time and practice
- ❖ Always try your best

Medical Injuries and Supplies (Healthcare)

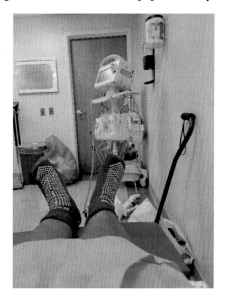

Medical Injuries and Medical Supplies

What is an injury?

An injury is something that causes hurt, pain, or a problem.

A **medical injury** is a problem on the body. For example, a broken arm.

Medical supplies are things to help heal an injury or assist a person with an injury.

Examples of medical supplies

Crutches **hospital gown**   **cane**   **arm sling**   **band aid**

Crutches: used to support a person's weight while trying to walk.

Hospital gown: a loose-fitting robe to cover the body for people getting medical procedures.

Cane (also called a walking stick): a stick that helps a person walk.

Arm sling: a medical device to help support an injured arm by limiting its movement. This is common for shoulder and elbow injuries too.

Band aid: a small band (sometimes called *tape*) to cover a wound

Did you ever use any of these medical supplies? If yes, write the name of the supplies.

_____

Read the conversation and answer the questions

Mira: Oh no! What happened to you?

Jose: I was in a car accident.

Mira: I'm so sorry. How do you feel?

Jose: I feel really bad. My arm is **broken**, my back hurts, and my foot is **sprained**.

Mira: Wow. What did the doctor say?

Jose: I have to stay home, take lots of medicine, and rest.

Mira: Can you go outside?

Jose: Yes, but I need to wear a **back brace** and use **crutches.**

What happened to Jose?

What are his injuries?

What medical supplies is Jose using?

TRUE or FALSE

Mira feels bad for Jose. _____

Jose doesn't need to take medicine. _____

A back brace is something you use for an arm or a leg. _____

A **back brace** is a brace that supports the back. This is used for people who have back problems or back injuries.

Surgery is a medical procedure people have when there's a medical problem, or injury.

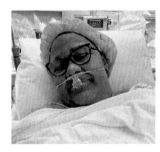

Teacher Dara uses a back brace. She had surgery on her lower back.

Did you have surgery? If yes, what kind of surgery did you have?

_____

Help! Call 911! Read the conversation and answer the questions

Thomas: Hey. Are you alright?

Deema: Ouch! No, I am not. I fell down the stairs.

Thomas: Can you stand up?

Deema: No, I can't. I can't move my legs.

Thomas: Okay, I'm going to get help. Stay calm.

Deema: Ooh…this hurts so much.

911 Operator: 911, what's your emergency?

Thomas: Yes, there's a lady who fell down stairs and can't get up.

911 Operator: Is she awake? Can she move?

Thomas: Yes, she's awake, but can't move her legs.

911 Operator: What is her address?

Thomas: Um, 913 East 9th Street, 1st floor.

911 Operator: Okay, help is on the way. Stay on the phone with me until help arrives.

Thomas: Okay, I will. The lady is in a lot of pain. She is crying.

What is wrong with Deema?

Why did Thomas call 911?

Where is Thomas and Deema?

What did the 911 Operator tell Thomas to do?

Why is it important to call 911?

DARA SAYS!

- ❖ Always follow the doctor's instructions when you have an injury
- ❖ Most doctor's offices or hospitals will give the patient the medical supplies he/she needs. For some medical supplies like crutches, the doctor or nurse will show the patient how to use them
- ❖ Medical supplies are usually covered by health insurance or paid by the patient
- ❖ Always follow the instructions on when and how often to use the medical supplies. Ask your doctor questions if you're unsure
- ❖ Try to remain calm when calling 911. Speak clearly and listen to the operator's instructions

Credit versus Debit (Money)

Answer the questions

Do you like money? _____

Do you prefer credit or debit? _____

What is the difference between *credit* and *debit*?

Credit and debit are sources of money to make purchases and transactions.

Purchases mean to buy something. Transactions mean how to pay for something.
For example: money or credit or debit cards

Let's look at an example of a **credit card bill** and a **bank statement**

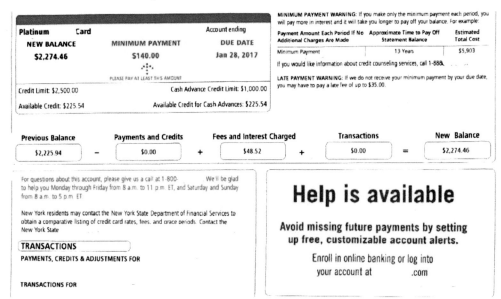

Look at the credit card statement and answer TRUE or FALSE

Available credit is $225.54 _____

The new balance is $2,374.47 _____

The payment due date is January 28, 2017. _____

The minimum payment is $200.00. _____

Billing cycle: the billing period between billing statements. A billing period or cycle is usually a month (30 or 31 days).

Interest: a percentage that is added to any item you buy. You receive a credit card bill that shows the amount of *money spent* (account balance), *the minimum payment* (amount of money you pay if you cannot pay the full balance), and *the due date for payment* (time you **must** pay your bill).

Do you pay your credit card bill by the **due date**? Why or why not?

Do you pay the **minimum payment** or t**he full balance**? Why or why not?

Look at the bank statement and answer the questions

TRANSACTION DETAIL	(continued)		
DATE	DESCRIPTION	AMOUNT	BALANCE
11/09	ATM Check Deposit 11/07 1	941.94	5,852.09
11/09	Card Purchase With Pin 11/07	-4.25	5,847.84
11/09	Card Purchase With Pin 11/07	-6.83	5,841.01
11/09	Card Purchase 11/07	-54.92	5,786.09
11/09	Card Purchase 11/07	-4.74	5,781.35
11/09	Card Purchase 11/09	-12.24	5,769.11
11/09	Card Purchase With Pin 11/08	-6.60	5,762.51
11/09	Acorns Invest Transfer	-20.00	5,742.51
11/10	Card Purchase 11/08 8000	-30.27	5,712.24
11/10	Card Purchase 11/09 8000	-8.59	5,703.65
11/10	Card Purchase 11/09 8000	-6.00	5,697.65

How many purchases were made using a debit card on 11/09? _____

What was the amount of the *check deposit*? _____

How many card purchases were made on 11/10? _____

What was the *last* balance on this bank statement? _____

Read the conversation between the customer and Cash-and-Pay Bank and answer the questions

Customer: Excuse, may I speak to a representative?

Bank representative: Yes, my name is Tim, how may I help you?

Customer: I am very upset! I received my bank statement in the mail and it shows I have 0 balance!

Bank representative: Did you make any recent transactions?

Customer: Yes, I made 5 transactions. The last one was on December 7th.

Bank Representative: Okay, let me take a look at your account. May I have your account number?

Customer: I don't remember my account number.

Bank Representative: May I have your debit card?

Customer: Here you go.

Bank Representative: Okay, so I see here that you made 5 transactions, and you had a balance of $2,480. Now I see there was another transaction on December 13th in the amount of $2,480.

Customer: That's impossible! I didn't make any transactions after December 7th.

Bank Representative: Okay, we will have to do an investigation to see who authorized this last transaction.

Why did the customer go to Cash and Pay Bank?

What was the customer's balance on December 7th?

Why is the customer so upset?

What will the bank representative do to help the customer?

Did you ever have this happen to you? If so, what happened?

DARA SAYS!

- ❖ Always carefully read your credit card bill and bank statements
- ❖ If anything looks suspicious, contact your bank and the credit card company immediately!
- ❖ It is important to pay your bills on time. Depending on your bill payment schedule, you should try to pay *before* or *on* the due date. If not, you will pay a **late fee**
- ❖ A **late fee** is an additional amount of money added to your bill for late payments
- ❖ NEVER GIVE YOUR BANK OR CREDIT INFORMATION TO A STRANGER! There are a lot of scams that will find ways to steal your information and your money

Scams

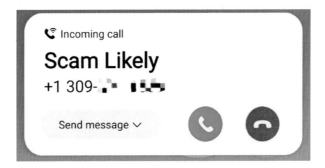

Can you read this?

Hi my name is fhejsnt sjsjkle and whywnnb xzxvcxzv $40000!!! Please call me back @123456789011 Bye, Ms. Wenzdie Joveusncitmeihh

What is wrong with this message?

_____

_____

_____

What does *scam* mean?

A scam means something that is NOT true, dishonest, fraud. Scams are messages through phone, email, mail, or social media, to steal your information and your money.

What do scams look like? Look at the 2 messages and name something that is wrong.

Saturday, October 15

Your package has arrived at the distribution center, delivery is suspended since wrong house number. fill in the required information: https:// 1:02 PM

_____

The world bank has
transferred your total
fund of 15.5 million USD
via western union since
3 days now and we have
not heard from you to
pick up your first payment
of $4,500 dollars Kindly
Contact HON. ⚹⚹⚹⚹⚹⚹
KLEIN from   ☆
union to pick up your
first payment $4,500

Where do you find scams? What do they look like?

Scams come in text messages, phone calls, emails, social media, and mail.

Scams look like the following:

- ❖ Misspellings in the message
- ❖ Fake phone numbers, email addresses, or addresses
- ❖ Requesting for money or offering large amounts of money in exchange for your personal information
- ❖ Bad language or threats
- ❖ Fake names and job titles
- ❖ False promises (example: Transfer $500 into account 12345678 to receive 2 million dollars
- ❖ Fake **sweepstakes (contests)** entries or free products in exchange for money
- ❖ "Kings" or "Princes" from foreign countries that are offering you large sums of money

Do you receive scams? What kind of scams did you receive and where (text message, email, mail, phone call or social media?)

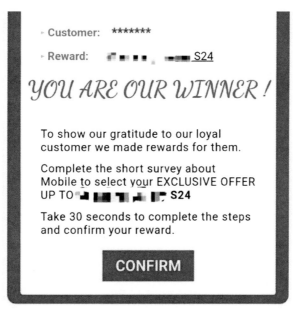

To show our gratitude to our loyal customer we made rewards for them.

Complete the short survey about Mobile to select your EXCLUSIVE OFFER UP TO ▪▪▪▪ S24

Take 30 seconds to complete the steps and confirm your reward.

CONFIRM

Read the phone conversation and answer the questions

Sue: Hello?

Viktor: Hi, is this Sue?

Sue: Yes, speaking.

Viktor: Sue, this is your lucky day! My name is Viktor from Amazing Mobile Phones and you are our winner for 1 million dollars!

Sue: Really? I can't believe it!

Viktor: Believe it Sue! Your name was selected from our contest and now you are 1 million dollars richer!

Sue: Wow! I still can't believe it!

Viktor: Believe it! Now Sue, in order to claim your prize, I need some information from you okay?

Sue: Sure.

Viktor: Great! I need your first and last name, date of birth, home address, email password, and bank account number to deposit your 1 million dollar prize.

Sue: That's a lot of information. I don't feel comfortable giving my bank account information over the phone.

Viktor: You have to give me your information to receive your prize. You want the 1 million dollars, don't you?

Sue: Well…

Who called Sue? _____

What is the name of the company the caller is from?

_____

What did the caller tell Sue?

_____

How does Sue feel about what the caller told her?

_____

What information did the caller ask from Sue?

_____

_____

Is this real or a scam? Why?

_____

_____

TRUE or FALSE: This is a REAL email message

You have (1) package waiting for delivery.

Verification needed!

Unfortunately, we were not able to deliver the postal package you ordered because the recipient's address was not correct.

Name:	▪▫▪ ▫▪▫
Email :	▪ ▫▪▫▪▫@gmail.com
Date:	2024/07/11
Tracking ID:	US-9357120622
Status:	Pending verification

Click here to verify

DARA SAYS!

- ❖ Be careful when receiving messages from people you don't know. Never send personal information or money to strangers
- ❖ Don't answer phone calls from numbers you don't recognize
- ❖ Many **scammers** (people who scam people) use different ways to convince you to give them your personal information, especially your bank account number or personal ID or social security number (these numbers identify who you are and where you are from)
- ❖ Never give your personal information over the phone UNLESS it is from your bank or a company you trust AND it is to verify who you are
- ❖ Scammers are NOT good spellers! Always check for misspellings in texts, mail, and emails. Delete it!

Warning Signs and Instructions

Warning Signs versus Instructions

What is the difference between a warning sign and instruction?

A **warning sign** tells us to pay attention.

An **instruction** sign tells us to do something.

Caution means to pay attention. What does **restricted area** mean?

Look at the signs and write **warning** or **instruction**

 a.

 b.

 c.

 d.

a. _____

b. _____

c. _____

d. _____

Matching: Match the sign with the correct meaning

Example: This sign means to stay away from area because it's dangerous.

1. This sign means not to exit
2. This sign means area is dangerous
3. This sign means to clean up after your dog
4. This sign means to leave immediately, there is a fire
5. This sign means you will be watched by a video camera

 _____

 _____

 _____

 _____

 _____

Read the conversation and answer the questions

Student A: I'm having a nice time exploring the city.

Student B: Me too! I am new here and I don't know many places.

Student C: I love the weather here. It's not too cold, but not too hot.

Teacher Dara: I agree with all of you.

Student A: Teacher, I see a sign. What does it mean?

Teacher Dara: Let's get closer to see what it is.

Student C: Uh oh, we can't walk there.

Student B: Why not?

Student C: Because it says, "danger" so we can't go to it.

Teacher Dara: It's okay, I will read the sign from here.

Student A: It's okay Teacher, I'll tell you!

Student C: Wait! It says, "Do not walk on grill slippery when wet."

Student A: I'm standing on the grill and it's not slippery.

Student B: But you don't know that and you can slip and fall down.

Teacher Dara: That's right. It's better to be cautious than to take a chance and get hurt.

Do you think student A was right to walk on the grill? Why?

Do you always follow the warning signs? Why or why not?

Create your own sign: In the box below, draw a sign for your home, workplace, or school. Make the message simple and easy to read. Choose the colors you want to use for your sign. Decide if your sign will be a WARNING or an INSTRUCTION sign.

Why is this sign important to you?

DARA SAYS!

- ❖ Always pay attention to warning and instruction signs. They will help you to stay safe
- ❖ Some signs will only have letters or a picture. Certain colors will mean it's a warning or an instruction. For example: RED=warning and YELLOW=instruction
- ❖ Lights are added to many warning signs for safety. Orange lights are used for construction signs.

Street Problems

What is wrong in this picture?

_____

What is wrong in this picture?

_____

Street problems are things that are wrong or dangerous for people. They can cause people to fall, get sick, or cause car accidents.

This is a broken street light. Why is this a problem?

_____

_____

Look at the picture. Read the conversation and answer the questions

Donny: Ouch!

Marissa: Hey, are you okay?

Donny: I was walking and talking on my phone. Next minute I know, I stepped on something sharp and fell down!

Marissa: Oh no! There's glass everywhere! Are you hurt?

Donny: Aww, I cut my foot and my left hand is bleeding.

Marissa: Okay, let me call 911.

Donny: No, no need for that. I can get up.

Marissa: You can't get up. Your foot is bleeding a lot! You need to get to a hospital. I'm calling 911.

1- What happened to Donny?

2- Was there a warning sign posted? _____

TRUE or FALSE:

Marissa fell on the glass too. _____

Donny wanted Marissa to call 911. _____

Donny fell down and cut his leg and left hand. _____

This is a **warning sign**. A <u>warning sign</u> means caution, to warn people to pay attention. This sign means to watch your step, to pay attention.

Do you think this sign would have prevented Donny from falling on the broken glass? Write YES or NO and why?

<u>Look at the pictures and write down the problem</u>

_____

_____

_____

_____

_____

 This is a **sewer**. A sewer is a system of pipes that removes waste (sewage) and wastewater from buildings and houses. This keeps the environment clean and safe for public health.

When there's a storm, sewers can get clogged and sanitation workers have to drain and clean the sewer grate.

Read the TV advertisement. Use the words below to fill in the blanks

Beware! The next time you're walking on the _____, or driving on the _____, beware of the potholes! Be on pothole patrol and pay attention to the potholes on the sidewalks and streets. They can be big or small. They will make you _____! _____ falls inside them, rats hide in them, and ice covers them. Sometimes, you can't see the potholes, but they are always there. What do you do? _____, look around, and _____ to the_____. You don't be a _____ to the next pothole!

Garbage- trash

Street- a road to drive a car, ride a bike, or cross to get to a sidewalk

Sidewalk- a path for people to walk

Fall- to move down quickly and unexpectedly

Pay attention- to be aware

Warning signs- signs to warn people from danger

Look down- to look down at something

Victim- a person that is injured, harmed, or killed

DARA SAYS!

- ❖ Always pay attention to warning and instruction signs. They will help you to stay safe
- ❖ If there are no warning signs, pay attention to the sidewalk, the street, and your surroundings

- ❖ Never walk on ice or on a pothole, even if it is small. You can trip and fall.
- ❖ Never drive over a pothole. Sometimes, this is unavoidable on highways or on streets with a lot of traffic. Try to avoid big potholes, because they can damage your car

How to read a newspaper article

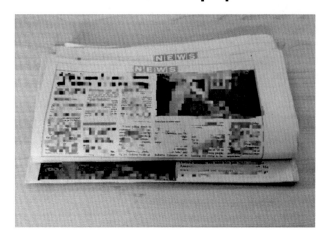

What is a newspaper?

A publication about current events (news), usually printed on paper or digitally online.

<u>Let's look at the article and learn the different parts of a newspaper article</u>

The Applied ESL Newspaper
New Supermarket Makes A Big Impression on Brooklyn Neighborhood

Bedrock Supermarket adds flavor to 10th Avenue neighborhood
Brooklyn, New York
May 12, 2014
Dara K. Fulton

The Bedrock Supermarket on 785 10th Avenue, opened its doors today. This grand opening is a nice comeback for business owner who is known in the neighborhood as "Mr. B." Mr. B also owns Center One discount store next door, which has been struggling with heavy competition from nearby businesses. This supermarket, according to Mr. B, will offer something new, a fish market. With a doorman opening the door for customers to friendly staff, this supermarket is off to a great start. There are fresh produce, dairy products, and name-brand items including some from different countries. The aisles are clean and there's a lot of space between the aisles. Don't see something you want? No problem. Ask Mr. B and he will order what you want. Both stores are open seven days a week. When I asked Mr. B how he feels about today's grand opening, he said, "I am grateful this is finally happening."

This is a chart of parts of a newspaper

We are only going to focus on the parts of the article in a newspaper

Name of newspaper: The Applied ESL Newspaper

Headline: Large printed words on top of a newspaper

Title of article: name of the article

Dateline: Location and date the article was written

Staff writer: person who wrote the article

Body: Main content, what the article is about

Main Idea: what the article is about

Answer the questions about the article

1- What is the **headline**?

_____

2- Who is the **staff writer**? _____

3- What is the **title** of the article?

_____

4- What is the **main idea** of the article?

_____

_____

_____

_____

5- What is the **dateline**? _____

6- What is the **name of the newspaper**? _____

Read this article from an English as a Second Language (ESL) student

Name of newspaper: Level 4 Writer's Workshop
My experience learning in the Writer's Workshop
Donald Cheng
Date: August 9, 2005

I'm a student of Level 4 Writer's Workshop class for six weeks. This course is on every Tuesday. The instructor is Dara K. Fulton. She is a very nice teacher. Every time she always gives the class a good atmosphere to make all the students interested to learn what she teaches and always encourages us to do this to answer more questions. Therefore, I feel I got more progress, especially recently she teaches us how to read the newspaper. This is my favorite because the words on the newspapers are very useful. Sometimes there is special news on the newspaper (Chinese) but it's not enough for me. So, I also buy the English too. I like to read them both. Of course, reading the newspaper is more different than book. There are a lot of hard words that I might not understand. So, I like to learn.

You Try: Write an article about your experience learning English. Use the articles to guide you

- ❖ What is your article's title?
- ❖ What is your name?
- ❖ The date of the article?
- ❖ What is the main idea?

Title: _____

Name: _____

Date: _____

Main idea of article

_____

_____

Article

_____

_____

_____

_____

_____

_____

_____

_____

_____

_____

_____

_____

_____

_____

_____

_____

_____

_____

_____

_____

_____

_____

_____

_____

_____

_____

_____

_____

_____

DARA SAYS!

- ❖ Newspapers help keep us informed. Whether paper or online, newspapers tell us what is happening in the world
- ❖ Reading articles help build our reading skills and learn new words
- ❖ The more you read articles, the easier it will be to find and understand the main idea

Recreational Places

What does recreation mean?

Recreation means an activity you enjoy doing in your free time.

Recreational places are places to relax and enjoy yourself.

Examples of recreational places:

Playground   Beach   Park

What recreational places do you like to visit?

_____

_____

_____

_____

_____

Read the conversation and answer the questions

Misty: Hey Rishi, do you want to go to the park today?

Rishi: Sure, which park do you want to go to?

Misty: I was thinking, we could go to McGee Park on 1st Avenue.

Rishi: Oh, I love that park. I go there on my lunch break.

Misty: Great! Do want to have lunch there today?

Rishi: Sounds good! There's a nice deli in the area. They sell the best sandwiches!

Misty: Do they make the all meat sandwich; chicken, beef, and ham sandwich with cheese and lettuce and tomato?

Rishi: Yes they do! I was going to have the tuna fish sandwich but…

Misty: Okay, we will meet at 1 pm and get the all meat sandwich. Then we will walk to the park.

Rishi: Okay, but don't forget the napkins. That sandwich can be messy.

1- What is the name of the park Misty and Rishi are going to?

_____

2- Where is the park located? _____

3- What kind of sandwich did Misty ask Rishi about?

_____

4- What time will Misty and Rishi meet? _____

5- What did Rishi tell Misty to bring? _____

TRUE or FALSE

Rishi has never been to McGee park. _____

Misty and Rishi will go to the deli first before going to the park. _____

Do you like to eat lunch at the park? Why or why not?

Read the radio announcement and answer TRUE or FALSE

Good morning! Don't let the sun fool you. Today we are expecting a **major thunderstorm** by afternoon time. Heavy rain and strong **wind gusts** will cause rough waves and strong winds. The temperature is 70 degrees now, but it will drop to 50 degrees by the time the storm starts. The beach may look nice now, but it will quickly become a dangerous place. There will be no **lifeguards on duty** today so no swimming is allowed. Do not go into the water. And most of all, stay safe.

1- It's a nice day to go to the beach. _____

2- There will be no thunderstorms today. _____

3- No swimming is allowed. _____

4- Lifeguards will be on duty. _____

5- The temperature will drop to 50 degrees. _____

6- You can go to the beach today. _____

Vocabulary

Major: something that is very big

Thunderstorm: A strong storm that involves thunder and lightening

Wind gusts: strong wind speeds

Lifeguards: people who are trained to rescue people who cannot swim or is drowning

On duty: at work

DARA SAYS!

- ❖ Always pay attention to the weather before going to a recreational place
- ❖ If there are any warning signs or announcements, follow the rules. It can save your life
- ❖ When eating at recreational places, always clean up any messes—never leave garbage behind. Throw your garbage in a garbage can
- ❖ Always pay attention to your surroundings—never go to a place that is unsafe. If you feel uncomfortable, leave immediately!

Going to the Movies

What is a movie?

A movie (also known as a film or a motion feature) is a visual of moving images that tells a story. We watch movies at home or in a movie theater.

There are different types of movies:

* ❖ Comedy- funny movie
* ❖ Action- exciting, lots of moving scenes
* ❖ Drama- a story that grabs your attention; full of emotions
* ❖ Horror- scary, unexpected events that makes you feel afraid
* ❖ Documentary- a story about a person's life or a story about an event in history

What kind of movies do you like? Why do you like them?

Do you prefer to watch movies in a movie theater or at home?

"I want to see the new movie Dara Says!" Read the conversation and answer the questions

Nelson: I'm so excited to see the new movie *Dara Says!*

Kelly: Me too, I hear it's a funny comedy.

TJ: It already received great **reviews**. Do you all have your tickets?

Marisol: No, I don't have a ticket.

Kelly: Girl, why not?

Marisol: I don't like buying my tickets online. I don't want anyone stealing my information!

Nelson: No one wants your information...you don't have no money!

Kelly: Haha good one Nelson!

TJ: Now now guys, let's stand on line so Marisol can buy her ticket.

Marisol: Thank you TJ! Nelson, you are welcomed to buy my ticket since I don't have no money.

1- What is the name of the movie the friends want to see?

_____

2- What type of movie is *Dara Says!* ?

_____

3- Who doesn't have a movie ticket?

_____

4- A **review** is an opinion about a movie. What reviews did *Dara Says!* get?

_____

Matching: Match the correct word with the picture

    a. Popcorn stand
    b. Movie theater seats
    c. Movie advertisement
    d. Movie ticket
    e. Place to order a movie ticket
    f. Rules of the movie theater
    g. Movie screen

MOVIE TICKET

R 01/25/2020
Sat 06:55 pm

Theatre 14
$14.00

CSH - ▦ - 24BBOXU6

01/25/2020 07:01 pm
Ticket: 00905195/002

_____   _____

NOW SHOWING

DARA SAYS!

THE LANGUAGE
ADVENTURE BEGINS!

February 6

SEE 3 MOVIES
A MONTH

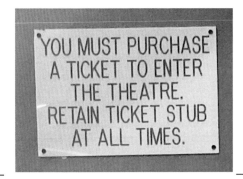

YOU MUST PURCHASE
A TICKET TO ENTER
THE THEATRE.
RETAIN TICKET STUB
AT ALL TIMES.

Advertisement for a new movie

TRUE or FALSE

The movie will open on April 1, 2025. _____
The name of the movie is *The Baby and Her Flowers.* _____
The movie is a horror movie. _____
The movie is a drama. _____
The movie is will come out in 2026. _____

DARA SAYS!

- ❖ Always check the time and date on your movie ticket
- ❖ Make sure you get to the movie theater early to buy your ticket, popcorn, or to use the restroom
- ❖ Follow the rules of the theater! Turn off your phone or put it on vibrate so you don't disturb the customers

- ❖ Never answer your phone inside the theater! You may be asked to leave because you are talking during the movie
- ❖ Some movie theaters have a **matinee (early movie times)** for people who want to watch the movie early
- ❖ Never leave garbage in the movie theater. Throw it away in a garbage can

APPENDIX A

Grammar points

Parts of Speech

Noun: people, places, things, animals, or an idea
Pronoun: replaces a noun
Example: I, me, you, we, us, they, them, he, his, she, her, it
Possessive pronouns (use to show ownership): my, his, her, our, their, theirs, your, yours
Example: My book. Her book. Your book. Their book. Our book.
Verb: an action word
Example: talk, listen, dance, watch, play
Adjective: a word that describes a noun
Example: beautiful, ugly, big, small, tall, short
Adverb: a word or phrase that describes, modifies, or quantifies an adjective, verb, or adverb. It can also express time, place, or a circumstance
*Most adverbs end in -ly
Example: really, randomly, abruptly, financially, quickly
For time (when and where something happened) or circumstances: here, often, there, everywhere, outside, inside, now, today, tomorrow, later
Preposition: connects a noun to another word
Example: at, after, to, on, but
Conjunction: joins sentences, words, or clauses together
Example: and, but, when
Example sentences: **When** I go to the doctor, I feel better.
We bought two shirts, three ties, **and** one coat.
He wants to go to school, **but** he doesn't feel well.

The is a definite article to talk about something specific. It is used before a noun
Interjection: short words or words with exclamation that are sometimes put in a sentence.
Example: Hi! Ouch! Oh! Well
Example sentence: Ouch! That hurts.

BE VERBS [am, is, are]

<u>BE verbs</u> are verbs that describe an action from people or things.

Subject + BE verb

I	**am**
You	**are**
We	**are**
They	**are**
He	**is**
She	**is**
It	**is**

Example: I am happy. He is hungry. We are tired.

Contractions

I am	**I'm**
You are	**You're**
We are	**We're**
They are	**They're**
He is	**He's**
She is	**She's**
It is	**It's**

(') is called an apostrophe
Use an apostrophe (') to make a contraction.

Negative:
Use *not* to make things negative
Example: I am *not* happy. We are *not* hungry. She is *not* tired.

Simple Present Tense and verbs in the third person (-s, -es, -ies)

We use the present tense when talking about things happening now.

Verb: talk

I	talk
You	talk
We	talk
They	talk
He	talks
She	talks
It	talks

With most verbs, we use **–s** when talking in the third person (he, she, it)
Example: Eat
He eat**s**, She eat**s**, It eat**s**

Verbs that have the following sounds: **s, z, ch, sh, x**, add **–es**
Example: Kis**s**= kisses
He kiss**es**, She kiss**es**, It kiss**es**

Buz**z**=buz**z**es
He buzz**es**, She buzz**es**, It buzz**es**

Tea**ch**=teaches
He teach**es**, She teach**es**, It teach**es**

Fini**sh**= finishes
He finish**es**, She finish**es**, It finish**es**

Fi**x**= fi**x**es
He fix**es**, She fix**es**, It fix**es**

Verbs that end in –y can also change to **–s** when it ends in one *vowel* + y
Example: play
"a" is a vowel
Play= plays
He plays, She plays, It plays

Verbs that end in –y can change into **–ies** if it ends with a *consonant* + y
Example: cry
"r" is a consonant
Cry= cries
He cr**ies**, she cr**ies**, it cr**ies**

Irregular verbs: verbs that do not follow the same rules as regular verbs.

Present	Past
go, goes	went
do, does	did
be	was, were
see	saw
eat	ate
become	became
feel	felt
fall	fell
break	broke
come	came
hurt	hurt
choose	chose
cut	cut
have, has	had
know	knew
lay	laid
give	gave
get	got
forgive	forgave
begin	began
drink	drank
bring	brought
make	made
read	read
let	let
lie	lay
hear	heard
meet	met
leave	left
run	ran
pay	paid
quit	quit
sell	sold
send	sent
sit	sat
ride	rode
fight	fought
teach	taught
steal	stole
understand	understood
think	thought
write	wrote
take	took
spend	spent

sleep	slept
speak	spoke

Vowels: a, e, i, o, u and sometimes y
Consonants: all letters except vowels. Y is also a consonant

BE VERBS in the Past Tense [was, were]

BE verbs in the past tense are verbs that describe an action from people or things in the past.

Subject + BE verb

I	**was**
You	**were**
We	**were**
They	**were**
He	**was**
She	**was**
It	**was**

Example: I was happy. He was hungry. We were tired.

Negative

Use *not* to make things negative. Use *not* after the verb.

Example: I was *not* happy.
We were *not* hungry.
She was *not* tired.

Simple Past Tense
We use the past tense when talking about things that happened in the past.

Verb: talk
Add **–ed** to the end of verbs for the past tense

I	talked
You	talked
We	talked
They	talked
He	talked
She	talked
It	talked

Verbs ending in **-e** (the –e is silent), add **–d**
Example: phone= phone**d**
*I phoned my friend. (British English)
I called my friend. (American English)

Close= close**d**
They closed the book.

Verbs ending in a *vowel*+ y, add **-ed**
Example: play= play**ed**
We played the game.

Verbs ending in a consonant+ y, add **-ied**
Example: marry= marr**ied**
She married her boyfriend.

Present Continuous
Present continuous is when something is happening now.

Subject + BE verb (am, is, are) + verb + -ing

Example: listen
I + am + listening.

Example: try
She + is + trying.

*Verb does not change in the third person.

Example: read
You + are + reading.

*Example: go
We use *going* with a <u>noun</u> (place) or verb (action)

I + am + going + to + <u>the supermarket</u>. (noun)

*to is a preposition that connects with the <u>noun</u>

They + are + going + <u>to listen</u>. (verb)

*Example: do
We + are + doing + <u>work</u>
We use *doing* with a <u>noun</u>

Negative
Use *not* to make things negative. Use *not* after the verb.

Example: I am *not* listening.
She is *not* trying.
You are *not* reading.
I am *not* going to the supermarket.
We are *not* doing work.

Past Continuous
Past continuous is when something is happening in the past.

Subject + BE verb (was, were) + verb + -ing

Example: speak
They + were + speaking.

Example: teach
I + was + teaching.

*Example: go
He + was+ going + <u>to the bedroom.</u> (place)
I + was + going <u>+ to think</u> (action)
When we use *going*, we include a verb (an action) or a noun (place)

*Example: do
They + were + doing + <u>homework.</u> (noun)
She + was + doing + <u>laundry.</u>
When we use *doing*, we include a <u>noun</u>

Negative
Use *not* to make things negative. Use *not* after the verb.

Example: There were not speaking.
I was not teaching.
He was not going to the bedroom.
I was not going to think.

Future tense

We use the future tense when talking about something in the future (something that did not happen yet).
We use **will** and **be going to** for the future tense.

We do not change the verb when using **will** or **be going to**

subject + will + verb (no change)

Example: study
I + will + study.

Example: travel
They + will + travel

Example: watch
He + will + watch *TV*.

*Sometimes we can add a *noun* at the end of the sentence

Negative

Use **not** to make things negative. Use **not** after will.

Example: I will **not** study.
They will **not** travel.
He will **not** watch TV.

subject + be going to + verb (no change)

Example: see
We + are going to + see + <u>a movie</u>. (noun)

Example: listen
I + am going to + listen + <u>to music</u>.

Example: read
He + is going to + read+ <u>a book</u>.

When using **be going to**, we can add a noun at the end of a sentence

Negative

Use *not* to make things negative. Use **not** after the BE verb.

Example: We are **not** going to see a movie.
I am **not** going to listen to music.
He is **not** going to read a book.

Present Perfect Tense

We use the present perfect tense to talk about an event that happened in the past but the result is in the present.

Subject + have/has + past participle

Example: I *have* **been** to New York.
This means you went to New York sometime in the past.

Example: She *has* **talked** to her friend.
This means she talked to her friend sometime in the past.

Negative

Use *not* to make things negative. Use **not** after have or has

Example: I have **not** been to New York.
She has **not** talked to her friend.

Subject	Have/ has	Past participle
I	have	These verbs have the –ed ending or are irregular
We	have	
You	have	
They	have	
He	**has**	
She	**has**	
It	**has**	

*Some verbs in past participle will be same in present and/or past tense

These are just a few examples of verbs in the past participle

Verb	Past Participle
talk	talked
listen	listened
walk	walked
study	studied
play	played
read	read
hurt	hurt
let	let
run	run
quit	quit
go	gone
be	been
do	done
see	seen

eat	eaten
become	become
begin	begun
give	given
choose	chosen
feel	felt
lay	laid
say	said
speak	spoken
pay	paid
take	taken
sell	sold
understand	understood
write	written
think	thought
teach	taught
sit	sat

We can include **time** *(since, for)* when talking in the present perfect

Subject + have/has + past participle + time

<u>Since</u> is used to state a specific time

I *have* <u>watched</u> the show *since* 10 o'clock.
He *has* <u>taught</u> class *since* yesterday.

<u>For</u> is used to state time (not specific)

We *have* <u>lived</u> in the United States *for* 12 years.
It *has* <u>been</u> raining *for* 3 days.

Negative
I have **not** watched the show *since* 10 o'clock.
He has **not** taught class *since* yesterday.
We have **not** lived in the United States *for* 12 years.
It has **not** been raining *for* 3 days.

'Wh' Questions

What- to ask about information
Example: What is your name?

When- to ask about time (time, day, week, month, year)
Example: When is the doctor's appointment?

Who- to ask about a person or people
Example: Who is the teacher?

Where- to ask about place
Example: Where is the restaurant?

Why- to ask about a reason
Example: Why are you applying for a job?

Which- to compare, to choose
Example: Which shirt do you want to buy?

Yes/ No Questions

Be verb (Am, Is, Are…?)

Example: **Am** I a teacher?
Answer: Yes you **are**. No, you **are not** (No you **aren't**)

Are you a student?
Yes I **am**. No, I **am not** (No, **I'm not**)

Is he a student?
Yes he **is**. No, he **is not**. (No, **he's not** *or* No, he **isn't**)

Is she a student?
Yes she **is**. No, she **is not**. (No, **she's not** *or* No, she **isn't**)

Do or Does…?

I	**do**
You	**do**
We	**do**
They	**do**
He	**does**
She	**does**
It	**does**

Example: **Do** you go to school?

Answer: Yes I **do**. No, I **do not** or No, I **don't**.

Does she go to school?
Yes she **does**. No, she **does not** or No, she **doesn't**.

Will…?

I	will
You	will
We	will
They	will
He	will
She	will
It	will

Example: **Will** you find a job?
Answer: Yes I **will**. No, I **will not** or No, I **won't**.

Will he find a job?
Yes he **will**. No, he **will not** or No, he **won't**.

Will they find a job?
Yes they **will**. No, they **will not** or No, they **won't**.

Will not= won't (contraction)

Modals

Modals are words that express permission, ability, obligation, possibility, advice, probability, prohibition (warning/cannot do something), lack of necessity (not a must)

Modal	Meaning
Can	Ability, permission, possibility
Could	Possibility, permission (polite), ability in the past
May	Permission, possibility, probability
Might	Permission (polite), possibility, probability
Will	Possibility (future)
Would	Permission (polite), possibility
Should, ought to	Advice, some obligation, conclusion
Shall	Make offers, suggestions, advice
Had better	advice
Must	Strong obligation, certainty
Must not	Prohibition
Need not	Lack of necessity/no obligation

We use *can, could, may, will, would,* and *shall* when asking questions.

Example: Can you help me?
Could you help me? (polite, more formal)
May I take your order? (polite, formal)
Will you go to the interview?
Would you like to buy the dress?
Shall we take the bus?

APPENDIX B
Vocabulary word definitions

Alphabet- English letters
Numbers- use to count things
Calendar- shows the month, year, days of the week, and dates
Season- different types of weather in a year
Weather- how the day feels (hot, cold, wet, or dry) and the temperature of the day
Temperature- the measure of hot or cold that is expressed in degrees Fahrenheit or Celsius.
Holidays- special occasions we celebrate during the year
Time- the hours and minutes in a day
Greetings- to greet, to say hello to someone
Formal- polite way of talking to someone you do not know, or someone who is in authority
Informal- a free, relaxed way of talking to someone you know
Conversation- two or more people talking to each other
Slang- informal English but more informal by the way we say words, expressions, and their meanings
New York City- a city in New York state in the United States
Body language- to communicate using your body (gestures) without speaking
Expressions- words or phrases to relay an idea
What's up with you?- How are you or Are you okay?
I got you- I am here for you
You frontin'- You are trying to impress others, not being honest
Don't sleep- to pay attention
Nah, I'm good- No, I'm fine
You feel me?- Do you understand me or Do you believe me?
Sis/Girl/Bro/Hommie- friend
My G- close friend
Workplace issues- problems at the workplace
Harassment- behavior that intimidates or harass people
Unfair treatment-to be treated not in a fair way
Low pay-pay that is below average
Discrimination- unfair treatment towards people based on race, ethnicity, age, gender, religion, or disability
No work advancement- no opportunity to advance into a higher work position
Lunch break- time period to have lunch
Favoritism- to favor/show likeness to one person or group of people over others
Prejudice- to have a negative opinion about people of different backgrounds
Bad boss-a person who doesn't care about his employees
Overtime- to work after work hours
Resign- to quit
File a complaint- to let a boss know that something is wrong or something was done to you at work

Letter of complaint- a letter to a supervisor or a boss about something that you are dissatisfied with at the job, or something that happened to you at the workplace

Job- work

Employment- paid work

Job position- the type of job

Full time- to work at least 40 hours a week

Part time- to work less than 40 hours a week

Job requirement- the skills, education, and experience needed for a job position

Skills- things you know how to do

Transferrable skills- the skills you have that can be used towards a job or career

Work experience (also known as *employment history*)- types of job positions you had

Resume- an outline of your work experiences, skills, and education

References- people who can talk about your work experience

Salary- money you receive from employer

Job advertisement (also called *ad* or *help wanted*)- an announcement about a job position

Abbreviations- short ways of writing words

Job search engine- an online site to find jobs

Job apps (applications)- a computer software or program that can be downloaded on computer or phone

Referred- to mention

Find out (found out)- to discover information

Interview- a conversation between a client and an employer about the job position the client is applying for

Qualified- to have the requirements for the job position

Interviewer- an employer, the person who conducts an interview

Interviewee- a person applying for a job

Tell me about yourself- to share current or past work experience, skills, and educational background

Strengths- things you are good at

Weakness- things you are not good at or need to improve

Aligned- to give support

Resign- to leave a job position by choice

Laid off- a company closes or a job position ends

Fired- to leave a job position by force

Study-to review any lesson or new things you learned in class

Text-to-voice-computer reads text messages in voice form

Highlight class notes- to use a highlighter (marker) to underline important notes

Flashcards: cards with vocabulary words or notes to help you study

Take notes- to write down what you hear in class

Organize notes for a class- use a notebook or a binder to organize your notes for each class

Set a study schedule- to pick a day (s) and time (s) to study

Quiet place to study- a place to study where there are no distractions

Study groups- to study with other people and help each other with questions

Take breaks- to take time to relax

Injury- something that causes hurt, pain, or a problem

Medical injury- a problem on the body. For example, a broken arm

Medical supplies- things to help heal an injury or assist a person with an injury

Crutches- used to support a person's weight while trying to walk.

Hospital gown- a loose-fitting robe to cover the body for people getting medical procedures

Cane (also called a walking stick)- a stick that helps a person walk

Arm sling- a medical device to help support an injured arm by limiting its movement. This is common for shoulder and elbow injuries too.

Band aid- a small band (sometimes called tape) to cover a wound

Broken- something that is not together, cracked, unable to use

Sprained- twist, a pull of a muscle or a body part

Back brace- a brace that supports the back. This is used for people who have back problems or back injuries

Surgery- a medical procedure people have when there's a medical problem, or injury

911- an emergency number in the United States

Debit card- a bankcard that you use to make purchases. Money is automatically taken out of bank account when purchase is made

Credit card- a card used to make purchases. Money is charged to card and payment is due at a certain time

Purchases- to buy things

Transactions- how to pay for something

Billing cycle- the billing period between billing statements

Interest- a percentage that is added to any item you buy

Late fee- an additional amount of money added to your bill for late payments

Bill- a statement about a purchase or a service you pay for

Late fee- additional amount of money added to your bill for late payments

Waive the late fee- customer is not charged a late fee

Bank- financial institution that allows people to deposit or withdrawal money

Deposit- to put money in an account

Withdrawal- to take money out of an account

Checking account- an account that allows the customer to write checks after he deposits money

Savings account- an account to save money

Bank teller- a person who helps customers at a bank

ATM- Automated Teller Machine (also called a cash machine) is a machine to withdraw money from a debit card

Ledger balance- the balance left in your account

Deposit slip- a slip you fill out to show the amount of money to deposit into a checking or savings account

Subtotal- the amount of money you want to deposit

Less cash- the amount of money to withdraw from the subtotal

Total- the total amount of money you want to deposit

Withdrawal slip- a slip you fill out to show the amount of money to take out from a checking or savings account

Pay to the order of- the person or company the check is going to.

Memo- to write additional information about the purpose of the check

Money order- an order of payment for a specific amount of money

Scam-something that is NOT true, dishonest, fraud

Scammers- people who scam people

Sweepstakes- contests

Street signs: things we see that gives us directions and instructions

Warning sign- tells us to pay attention.

Instruction sign- tells us to do something

Caution- to pay attention

Restricted area- an area you are not allowed to enter

Danger sign- an area that is dangerous

Exit- to leave

Not an exit- cannot leave

Curb your dog-clean up after your dog

Fire alarm- to leave immediately, there is a fire

Warning-Security camera in use- a hidden camera that protects a business or a home from criminal activity

Do Not Walk On Grill-Slippery When Wet- do not walk on grill (grate) when it is wet

Slippery- wet surface that makes it difficult to stand or walk on

Local Street Signs- gives directions on streets that are small, have lower speed limits, and instructions where people can walk, drive, or ride a bicycle

Highways- high speed roadways that connects cities and towns, have higher speed limits and more traffic

Highway signs- gives directions to drivers or warnings on the highway such as construction and weather warnings

Stop sign- to come to an end; no movement

Bicycles- vehicles that are made of two wheels, a handle bar, and pedals

No bicycles allowed sign- no bicycles permitted on street or sidewalk

Allowed- permit

Closed- a sidewalk or street not open

Traffic- vehicles that move on streets, roads, and highways

Signal Ahead- traffic must prepare to see the signals (red, yellow, green)

Speed limit- restriction of speed on a street

Exit-to leave a street or highway

Push to walk- a button for people to change the light from do not walk to walk

Speed bump- a bump to prevent speeding

Right of way- permission for cars or pedestrians to cross the street

Pedestrians- people

Walk signal- permission to cross the street

Do not walk sign- to stop

Light- the light that instructs pedestrians and cars to go, wait, or stop

Cross- to walk across a street

Jaywalking- to walk across the street without permission
Cyclists- people who ride bicycles
Miles per hour (mph)- the amount of speed
Photo enforced- photos taken of cars that break traffic rules
Construction or Work Ahead signs- signs that direct traffic when there is work on the street or highway; these signs are in orange color
Slow sign- to warn drivers to slow down
Flagger- a construction worker that directs traffic when there is work on the road
Detour- change in direction
Work zone- to let drivers know there is construction work ahead
Street problems- things that are wrong or dangerous for people
Sewer- a system of pipes that removes waste (sewage) and wastewater from buildings and houses
Garbage- trash
Street- a road to drive a car, ride a bike, or cross to get to a sidewalk
Sidewalk- a path for people to walk
Fall- to move down quickly and unexpectedly
Pay attention- to be aware
Warning signs- signs to warn people from danger
Look down- to look down at something
Victim- a person that is injured, harmed, or killed
Newspaper- a publication about current events (news), usually printed on paper or digitally online
Headline- Large printed words on top of a newspaper
Title of an article- name of the article
Dateline- Location and date the article was written
Staff writer- person who wrote the article
Body- Main content, what the article is about
Main Idea- what the article is about
Recreation- an activity you enjoy doing in your free time
Recreational places- places to relax and enjoy yourself
Major- something that is very big
Thunderstorm- a strong storm that involves thunder and lightening
Wind gusts- strong wind speeds
Lifeguard- people who are trained to rescue people who cannot swim or is drowning
On duty- at work
Movie- (also known as a film or a motion feature) is a visual of moving images that tells a story
Comedy- funny movie
Action- exciting, lots of moving scenes
Drama- a story that grabs your attention; full of emotions
Horror- scary, unexpected events that makes you feel afraid
Documentary- a story about a person's life or a story about an event in history
Popcorn stand- place to buy popcorn inside a movie theater
Movie theater seats- seats inside the movie theater
Movie advertisement- an announcement about an upcoming movie

Movie ticket- a physical or digital document that shows proof of purchase and allows you to enter the movie theater

Place to order a movie ticket- to buy a movie ticket

Rules of the movie theater- what you can and cannot do at the movie theater

Movie screen- the screen to watch the movie

Matinee- early movie times

APPENDIX C

Answers to exercises

Preview
Weather: write your own answer
Birthday: write your own answer
Time: 8 o'clock or 8:00
Informal English/Slang: write your own answers

UNIT 1-Workplace Issues

Match the scenarios with the vocabulary word:
1. prejudice, harassment, 2. favoritism, discrimination 3. favoritism, unfair treatment, 4. discrimination, unfair treatment, no work advancement

TRUE or FALSE
1. FALSE
2. FALSE
3. FALSE
4. TRUE
5. TRUE
6. FALSE
7. TRUE

Letter of complaint
1- Lilly Chan
2- Mr. Martinez and Ms. James
3- Prejudice, discrimination, harassment from co-workers, low pay, not allowed the same lunch break
4- To avoid the company from making the same mistakes; improve

Write letter of complaint- write your own answer to the complaint

UNIT 2-Ways to Study (Education)

Matching: 1- **C**, 2- **D**, 3- **B**, 4- A

What do you study? Write your own answer
How do you study? Write your own answer
What do you want to study? Write your own answer

You Try: Create a study schedule- Write your own answer
Write 3 ways you will study- Write your own answer
Do you like to study? Why or why not? Write your own answer

UNIT 3-Medical Injuries and Supplies (Healthcare)

Did you ever use any of these medical supplies? If yes, write the name of the supplies- write your own answer

Answers to questions from conversation
1- car accident
2- broken arm, back hurts, sprained foot
3- back brace and crutches

TRUE or FALSE
1- TRUE
2- FALSE
3- FALSE

Did you have surgery? If yes, what kind of surgery did you have?- write your own answer

Help! Call 911! Answers to questions
1- She fell down the stairs
2- Deema can't move her legs
3- 913 East 9th Street, 1st floor
4- Stay on the phone until help arrives
5- It helps save a life, and get help for people who are injured

UNIT 4 -Credit versus Debit (Money)

Do you like money? Write your own answer
Do you prefer credit or debit? Write your own answer

TRUE or FALSE
1- TRUE
2- FALSE
3- TRUE
4- FALSE

Do you pay your credit card bill by the due date? Why or why not?- write your own answer
Do you pay the minimum payment or the full balance? Why or why not?- write your own answer

Bank statement answers to questions

1- **6**, 2- **$941.94**, 3- **3**, 4- **$5,697.65**

Answers from conversation with bank teller

1- Customer's bank statement shows 0 balance

2- $2,480

3- Customer didn't make any transactions after December 7th

4- The bank will do an investigation about the last transaction

5- **Did you ever have this happen to you? If so, what happened?**- write your own answer

UNIT 5 -Scams

What's wrong with this message?
The message is not correct, it doesn't make sense

Scam message 1:
- Website doesn't look real
- Mail is always sent to an address, post offices don't need to ask for your address or personal information

Scam message 2:
- No one will send a large amount of money to a stranger
- Who is Klein? You don't know this person
- You never have to meet anyone to pick up money

Do you receive scam messages? What kind of scams did you receive and where?
Write your own answer

Answers to conversation questions

1- Viktor
2- Amazing Mobile Phones
3- Feels excited at first but later become concerned
4- First and last name, date of birth, home address, email password, and bank account number
5- Yes, because you don't know the person or caller; never give your personal information over the phone

TRUE or FALSE: FALSE

UNIT 6 -Warning Signs and Instructions

What does restricted area mean? An area you are not allowed to enter

Warning or Instruction: 1- Instruction 2- Warning 3- Warning 4- Instruction

Matching: 1- **4**, 2- **3**, 3- **1**, 4- **5**, 5- **2**

Do you think student A was right to walk on the grill? Why? Write your own answer

Do you always follow the warning signs? Why or why not? Write your own answer

Create your own sign: In the box below, draw a sign for your home, workplace, or school. Your sign picture

Why is this sign important to you? Write your own answer

UNIT 7 -Street Problems

What is wrong in this picture?

Picture 1- Garbage on the sidewalk
Picture 2- There are cracks on the street

Broken street light-Why is this a problem?
A broken street light is dangerous, because it can cause accidents, and people and cars won't know when to stop or go.

Answers to questions from conversation

1 Donny stepped on glass and fell down
2 No warning sign was posted

TRUE or FALSE

1- FALSE, 2- FALSE, 3- TRUE

Do you think this sign would have prevented Donny from falling on the broken glass? Write YES or NO and why?

No because Donny wasn't paying attention. He was on his phone.

Pictures of street problems

- Sidewalk is broken
- Street light fell and is upside down
- Sidewalk is being fixed, cannot walk on the sidewalk
- Lots of garbage on the sidewalk
- Snow and ice on the sidewalk

TV advertisement: fill in the blanks

1-sidewalk
2- street
3- fall
4- garbage
5- look down
6- pay attention
7- warning signs
8- victim

UNIT 8 -How to read a newspaper

Answers to questions about article

1- New Supermarket Makes a Big Impression on Brooklyn Neighborhood
2- Dara K. Fulton
3- Bedrock Supermarket Adds Flavor to 10th Avenue Neighborhood
4- A new supermarket opens in Brooklyn neighborhood. The owner, Mr. B owns both this supermarket and a discount store. He is happy because the supermarket will bring new customers and it can help keep the discount store open.
5- May 12, 2014
6- The Applied ESL Newspaper

You Try: Write an article about your experience learning English-Write your own answer

UNIT 9 -Recreational Places

What recreational places do you like to visit?- Write your own answer

Answers to questions from conversation

1- McGee Park
2- 1st Avenue
3- All meat sandwich
4- 1 pm
5- napkins

Do you like to eat lunch at the park? – Write your own answer

Radio announcement-TRUE or FALSE

1- FALSE, 2- FALSE, 3- TRUE, 4- FALSE, 5- TRUE, 6- FALSE

UNIT 10 -Going to the Movies

What kind of movies do you like? Why?- Write your own answer
Do you prefer to watch movies in a movie theater or at home?- Write your own answer

Answers to questions from conversation

1- Dara Says!
2- Comedy
3- Marisol
4- Good reviews

Matching

1- **D**, 2- **G**, 3- **A**, 4- **C**, 5- **E**, 6- **F**, 7- **B**

Advertisement for a new movie: TRUE or FALSE

1 FALSE
2 TRUE
3 FALSE
4 TRUE
5 TRUE

PREVIEW LESSON WORKSHEETS

Complete the alphabet chart

A		C	D			G	H		J
	L	M	N		P		R		T
U		W			Z				

Write the number

1 _____

2 _____

3 _____

4 _____

5 _____

6 _____

Write the lower case letter

A	B	C	D	E	F	G	H	I	J
K	L	M	N	O	P	Q	R	S	T

U	V	W	X	Y	Z

Write the number

10 _____

20 _____

30 _____

40 _____

50 _____

Look at the calendars and write the date

APRIL 2025

Sunday	Monday	Tuesday	Wednesday	Thursday	Friday	Saturday
		1	2	3	4	5
6	7	8	9	(10)	11	12
13	14	15	16	17	18	19
20	21	22	23	24	25	26
27	28	29	30			

_____

MAY 2025

Sunday	Monday	Tuesday	Wednesday	Thursday	Friday	Saturday
				1	2	3
4	5	6	7	8	9	10
11	12	13	14	15	16	17
18	19	20	21	(22)	23	24
25	26	27	28	29	30	31

_____

Days of the week: Fill in the blanks

M ____ n ____ ____ y

____ u ____ s ____ a ____

W ____ ____ ____ e s ___ a ____

____ h u ____ s ____ ____ ____

F ___ i d ___ ___

S ___ ___ u ___ d a ____

___ ____ ____ d ____ ____

Write the abbreviation

Monday _____   Friday _____

Tuesday _____   Saturday _____

Wednesday _____   Sunday _____

Thursday _____

Months of the year: Write the month

Jan _____   Jul _____

Feb _____   Aug _____

Mar _____   Sept _____

Apr _____   Oct _____

May _____   Nov _____

Jun _____   Dec _____

Write the correct month for each sentence

The <u>first</u> month of the year is _____

The <u>third</u> month of the year is _____

The <u>fifth</u> month of the year is _____

The <u>seventh</u> month of the year is _____

The <u>ninth</u> month of the year is _____

The <u>eleventh</u> month of the year is _____

What is today?

Write the date using ordinals

JUNE 2025

Sunday	Monday	Tuesday	Wednesday	Thursday	Friday	Saturday
1	2	3	4	5	6	7
8	9	10	11	12	13	14
15	16	17	18	19	20	21
22	(23)	24	25	26	27	28
29	30					

Today is _____

JULY 2025

Sunday	Monday	Tuesday	Wednesday	Thursday	Friday	Saturday
		1	2	3	4	(5)
6	7	8	9	10	11	12
13	14	15	16	17	18	19
20	21	22	23	24	25	26
27	28	29	30	31		

Today is _____

What is today?

Write the date using ordinals

NOVEMBER 2025

Sunday	Monday	Tuesday	Wednesday	Thursday	Friday	Saturday
						1
2	3	4	(5)	6	7	8
9	10	11	12	13	14	15
16	17	18	19	20	21	22
23	24	25	26	27	28	29
30						

Today is _____

DECEMBER 2025

Sunday	Monday	Tuesday	Wednesday	Thursday	Friday	Saturday
	1	2	3	4	5	6
7	8	9	10	11	12	13
14	15	16	17	18	19	20
(21)	22	23	24	25	26	27
28	29	30	31			

Today is _____

What is the season?

_____   _____

_____   _____

Choose the correct words to describe the weather

Rainy Hot Cold Cloudy Sunny Foggy Warm Cool

It is

It is

It is

It is

Use the words to describe the weather in the picture

Hot   Cold   Sunny   Snowy   Warm   Cool

Write the name and month of the holiday

_____

Write the name of the holidays and their months

Write the name of the holidays and their months

What time is it?

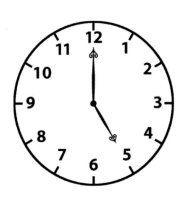

It is _____

It is _____

It is _____

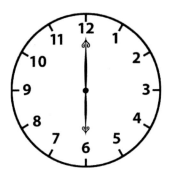

It is _____

What time is it?

It is _____

It is _____

It is _____

It is _____

Draw the time

Teacher Dara says:

TRY YOUR BEST

Made in United States
North Haven, CT
12 June 2025

69730345R00066